300+ Tax Deductions

For Self-Employed Individuals and Business Owners

All rights Reserved. No part of this e-book may be reproduced, stored or transmitted in any form or by any electronic means without written permission from the author.

Important Notice: While this book contain beneficial and accurate information, I cannot personally guarantee the information is correct or will be appropriate to your particular situation. Laws and regulation change frequently and are Laws and regulation change frequently and are subject to

differing interpretations. It is your responsibility to verify all information and all laws discussed in this book before relying solely on them. Nothing in this book will substitute for legal advice. You may want to obtain specific information from the IRS or a qualified person.

Any persons or entities intending to use this information should visit:

www.irs.gov and speak with a Tax Preparer for further application and information.

Introduction

One of the 1st questions people ask is "How can I pay as little taxes as possible?" Next is "What can I write off as a business owner?"

To make a complicated topic simple to understand, I have complied over 300+ tax deductions that you can legitimately use to reduce your taxes.

The IRS will not let you know when you have missed a deduction. That is up to you to make sure that you are taking advantage of all the many deduction available to you. Knowing what you can write off in the course of your business will help you plan accordingly throughout the year.

Disclaimer: The information in this e-book is for general information purposes only. These tax issues are complicated, and every situation is different, so you should consult your CPA/tax advisor.

300+ Deductions

Accounting Expenses

Tax Preparation, Accounting expenses, auditing expenses, and bookkeeping expenses are deductible business expenses.

Tax Preparation fees: Tax preparation, including preparing and filing

forms by a CPA, tax attorney, or tax adviser, for tax strategy and are business deductions.

Accountant/CPA/Financial Adviser

The services of a CPA, an accountant, or financial adviser for review of financial statements or business financial planning.

Bookkeeping Expenses: You can deduct all expenses for bookkeeping,

including those for a bookkeeper, or for bookkeeping and accounting software to help you or an employee do your bookkeeping.

Auditing

If you are a public corporation, you can deduct fees for an auditing firm.

Expenses for accounting for illegal activities are never deductible. You cannot deduct the cost of accounting software or the services of a tax preparer, for your personal tax return. Preparation of your Schedule SE for self-employment taxes is a personal tax expense, and it can't be deducted as a business expense.

You can't deduct fines and penalties for late filing or for underpaying your taxes,

so make sure you know the tax filing deadlines and that your tax preparer or tax software is accurate.

Advances

If you pay contractors, suppliers, professionals, and vendors, the advancement can be deducted

Advertising

Advertising expenses are deductible. Advertising is so broad, so I've listed some categories below:

- Costs of advertising materials: business cards, brochures, and web pages.
- Advertising in media: Ads, Media, Social Media Ad promotion, Pens with your
- business logo newspapers, TV, internet, cable, and magazines.
- Marketing activities such as direct marketing.
- Promotional and public relations expenses, and promotional items like mugs,
- caps, t-shirts, and pens.

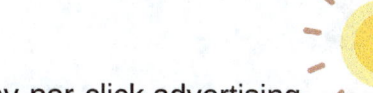

- Online advertising such as email newsletters, pay-per-click advertising, and SEO services
- Costs of advertising events such as a promoters, publicity campaign.

You can deduct the cost of putting an advertisement for your business on your car (business or personal), but you can't deduct the cost of driving your car around town as an advertising expense.

Alarms

Alarm systems can be ducted the year purchased. If there are monthly service fees and alarm rentals, fee is fully deductible.

Amortization

Intangible business assets, like intellectual property, customer base, and licenses, are amortized. The processes of depreciating and amortizing are basically the same. The value of the asset is determined, and the life of the asset is calculated by comparing it to other similar assets.

Intangible assets include:

- Goodwill.
- Going concern value.
- Workforce in place (that is, current employees, including their experience, education, and training)
- Business books and records, operating systems, or any other information base, including lists or other information concerning current or prospective
- customers.

A patent, copyright, formula, process, design, pattern, know-how, format, or similar item.
- A customer-based intangible, including customer base and relationships with customers.
- The value of future purchases due to relationships with vendors.
- License, permit, or other right granted by a governmental unit or agency.
- An agreement or covenant not to compete or non-compete agreement entered into in connection with the acquisition of an interest in a trade or business.
- A franchise, trademark, or trade name.
- A contract for the use of, or a term interest in any item in this list.
- Copyrights and patents, interests in films, sound recordings, books, or other similar property.
- Interests in a corporation, partnership, trust, or estate; in land or in certain financial contracts.
- Sports franchises
- Some computer software.
- Some corporate transaction costs.

Certain intangible assets are NOT considered to be intangibles, and may not be amortized over 15 years. The IRS has very strict guidelines relating to intangible assets. You should consult you CPA for specific says you cannot amortize assets in categories 1 through 8 if you created these assets, unless "you created them in acquiring assets that make up a trade or business or a substantial part of a trade or business."

Application Software
Better known as "apps". If purchased and it relates to business the fee is 100% deductible.

ATM Fees
Automatic teller Machine (ATM) are deductible.

Attorneys
Attorney fees are deductible. See *Professional fees* for more detailed description and exceptions.

Audits
The cost of auditing services or an audit by an accounting firm is deductible. Fees associated with hiring a CPA or Lawyer to defend your business in an IRS audit is deductible.

Automobiles
Whether you have a car that has been purchased by your business or you are using your personal vehicle for business purposes, you need to know which expenses are deductible. The IRS regulations for deducting business driving expenses apply to employees and business owners in different ways.
Business driving is a valid business activity. If a business owner drives for business purposes, the cost of driving is deductible. If the business pays the driving expenses of its employees, those costs are also deductible to the business. Before you deduct car expenses, be sure to consult with your CPA/tax advisor to ensure you are properly deducting this expense.

Awards
You can deduct the cost of employee awards from your business taxes, up to $400 for awards of tangible personal property (like a watch) for each employee each year. It includes service awards and safety awards.

Baby Sitting
See *Dependent care*

Bad debts

Credit card charges customers refuse to pay and bounced checks are deductible.

Bank Charges

Bank Charges, ATM Fees, bank services, check printing cost, penalties and credit card fees are all deductible.

Bankruptcy

Cost and related expenses of filing for bankruptcy are deductible.

Barter

There may be a time that you exchange or trade your business goods or services for someone else's goods or services; that is called a barter. You are allowed to deduct the cost of the merchandise you are giving away. However, if you are trading your services you are not allowed a deduction because you are cannot deduct the value of your own time.

You must capture the "Fair Market Value" of the goods and/or services you receive as business income. Fair Market value is what you would have normally paid for the goods or services in normal course of business.

Billboards

If you are renting or own a billboard you can deduct the expense. Rental cost for billboards is deductible. Billboards you own can be deducted the year of purchase or depreciated over time.

Bitcoins

Paying your business expenses in Bitcoin and other digital currencies are deductible exactly the same as expenses paid in the US dollar. The amount of the expense is the fair market value of the goods or services you are getting in exchange for the bitcoin.

Boats

Boats, if needed for your business, can be deducted the year of purchase or depreciated over several years.

Bodyguard

Bodyguard services is an ordinary and necessary expense of your business, it is a deductible expense.

Bonus

Bonuses for employers/owners are a legitimate business expense and can be deducted under certain circumstances. First, Let's take a look at bonuses for owners/shareholders:

- S Corporations can deduct bonuses for shareholders and owners, as long as they own their shares at the time the bonus is paid.
- C Corporations can only deduct bonuses for shareholders/owners who have a 50 percent or higher ownership at the time the bonus is paid.
- For sole proprietorships, partnerships, and limited liability companies (LLCs), bonuses are not deductible business expenses because the owners/partners/members are considered by the IRS to be self-employed. This is one situation in which having a corporation and being an employee of that corporation might result in more tax deductions.

Bonuses to employees are considered income and are taxable to the employee.

You must withhold income taxes and FICA taxes on employee bonuses (unless the employee is over the Social Security maximum for the year. If you decide to give your employees a bonus, you must give them the opportunity to change their withholding authorization (on Form W-4) for that paycheck, and change it back for subsequent paychecks. Many employees like to change their bonus check withholding, so they receive more of the bonus.

Bookkeeping

Certified Public Accountant (CPA), Bookkeeping, accounting, recordkeeping, bookkeeping software you purchased are deductible.

Booking agency fees/ Management

For Musicians, artist, entertainers, booking agents fees that are paid out of pocket are deductible. Books

Books

Books, Magazine, E-Book, Newsletters, newspapers are deductible.

Bounced Checks

Your customer checks bounce; deduct the amount of the check.

Boxes

If you have boxes, packaging materials, cartons, and other containers that holds the good you sell are considered part of your inventory, therefore this expense is apart of Cost of goods sold and is deductible.

Brokers Fee

Broker's fee to buy or sell real estate is added to the value of the real estate and depreciated.

Buildings

Buildings that you or your business owns are depreciated over time.

Building Improvements

Building improvements, renovations, renovations, remodeling, and repairs can be deducted.

Business Assets

Business Assets are possessions you use in your business such as equipment, machinery, tools, furniture, fixtures, office machines, computers, vehicles, buildings, Intangible assets (Trademarks, patents, copyrights, etc.) are deductible.

Business Cards

Business cards are deductible

Business Gifts

Your business can deduct no more than $25 of a gift to any one person each year, including employees.

Business Licenses

Business licenses, registrations, and similar fees are deductible.

Business Trips

Business trips are deductible, but there are many rules and restrictions.
See *Travel*

Bus

You can deduct the cost of using a bus for business, but with limitation.
See Automobiles

Campaign Contributions

Political contribution is not deductible

Cancellation Penalties

Cancelation penalties are deductible

Carrying Charges

A carrying charge is a service charge or financing charge for buying something overtime/installments. Carry charges are treated like interest charges and are deductible.

Cars

You can deduct the cost of using a car for business, or you can take a standard mileage rate, but with limitations. See *Automobile*.

Casualty Losses

Business losses from storm, fire, theft, vandalism, and shoplifting are sometimes deductible and sometimes not, depending on what was destroyed or stolen. There are different rules for different types of losses and different types of businesses, consult your CPA.

Cell Phones

If you use your cellular phone and Smartphone 100% of the time for business; it is 100% deductible. However, if your phone is used partly for business, you are required to deduct the percentage of the cost used for the business.

Charitable Contributions

You or your business can deduct any of the following:

- Cash contributions
- Gifts of property or equipment (called "in-kind" contributions)
- Mileage and other travel expenses incurred in working for a charitable organization, based on the IRS-designated standard mileage rate for charitable work.

You cannot deduct the value of your time or the time of your employees working as a volunteer for a charitable organization, such as time spent serving on a nonprofit board.

If you are a sole proprietor, your business taxes are filed on Schedule C of your personal Form 1040. Your business cannot make separate charitable contributions because the only way individuals can deduct these contributions is on Schedule A. That means you must be able to itemize the deductions to take them. The same is true for a single-member limited liability company since the single-member LLC files taxes as a sole proprietor.

If the partnership makes a charitable contribution, each partner takes a percentage share of the deduction on his or her personal tax return. For example, if the partnership has three equal partners and donates a total of $3,000 to charity in a year, the partners can each claim $1,000 in charitable deductions.

Child Care

See *Dependent care*

Classes

Many classes and education are deductible. See *Education*

Cleaning Services

Cleaning and janitorial services for the business premises are deductible. In addition, clothing used for cleaning and laundry services used exclusively for work are deductible if the clothing is unsuitable for street wear, such as uniform, costume or protective gear.

Closing cost

Closing cost include processing fees, broker commission, title, property taxes, insurance, termite reports, loan fees, transfer taxes, loan fees, points and other cost are deductible immediately. Others are deductible over a period of years. This can be complicated, Consult your CPA.

Clothing

Clothing used exclusively for work and unsuitable for street wear is deductible. Clothing with your company logo, uniform, costumes, protective gear are deductible.

Clubs

Membership fees and dues for clubs, associations and organizations may or may not be deductible, depending on the nature of the organization.

Coffee services

For all my coffee lovers, you will be delighted to know that your coffee services is a deductible office expense

Commissions & Fees

Commissions that you pay to acquire new customers who sign long-term contracts may have to be amortized over a period of years. Commissions that you pay to outside salespeople or companies and commissions paid for referrals, finders fees, and the like are deductible. Real estate commissions are added to the cost of real estate and depreciated over the life of the asset.

Commuting

You are not allowed to deduct commuting expenses from your home to your regular place of business and back. The IRS allows businesses to deduct expenses for business travel by owners and employees, but no deductions are allowed for commuting expenses. The rationale is that everyone commutes (travels to work), so commuting is not a business but a personal expense.

Compensation

Self-employed people cannot take a deduction for compensation you pay to yourself. See *Paying yourself.* Compensation paid to any independent contractors or other nonemployees is deductible.

Employers compensation to employees is deductible.

Corporations Owners of corporations are employees of their businesses. Your compensation is treated like any other employee wages.

Computers

Computers, monitors, printers can be deducted the year of purchase or deducted over the five years.

Condominium

Business Condominium that you rent or lease are deductible. Business Condominiums that you own are depreciated like any other business building. Condominium associations, management fees, and other charges are deductible if business related.

Conferences

Cost of conducting or attending business conferences are deductible. Including travel and meals. Meals are 50% deductible.

Consultants

Consultant fees are deductible.

Contractors

Contractor fees for new construction of a building is added to the cost of the building and depreciated.

Contracts

The cost of preparing a contract is deductible if it is not substantial.

Contribution

Money contributed to your own business is income or expense to your business, therefore, it is not deductible.

Conventions

Fee for attending a business convention is deductible. Travel and lodging expenses are deductible; meals are 50% off

Copies

Copies are a deduction

Copyrights

Copyright is amortized over 15 years.

Cost of Good Sold

Businesses can deduct the cost of inventory once the goods are sold.

Courier Service

Deductible!

Credentials

The cost of education to obtain a credential is deductible in some situations. See *Education*

Credit Cards

Making purchases for your business on a credit card is 100% deductible. If you are a sole proprietor or a single member LLC you can deduct purchases made on your personal credit card. Note, you can not include personal charges.

Partnerships, LLCs, Corporation and S-Corp should have a debit and credit cards in the business name to maximize tax deductions.

Credits

If you purchase goods/service and you receive a credit to reduce the cost, treat the credit like a discounted price.

Customer List

A customer list that you purchase is considered an intangible asset, which is amortized over 15 years.

Customs

Custom duties and all fees and taxes related to importing and exporting can be deducted.

Database

A database that you purchase is considered an intangible asset which is amortized over 15 years.

Day Care

See Dependent Care.

Day care Business: Expenses For running a day care business are deductible like the expenses of any other business, including meals served. If you operate your day care out of your home, see Home expenses for deductions allowed.

Debit Cards

Debit & credit card fees and expenses are handled the same.

Decorating

Decorating expenses are deductible.

Delivery Charges/ Shipping

Delivery charges incurred for goods you sell, business assets, weekly delivery services are deductible.

Demolition

The cost to demolish a building is added to the cost basis of the land. It cannot be deducted or depreciated.

Dependent Care

You can deduct up to 5,000 a year for child and dependent care for your own children or dependents. The deduction cannot exceed your net profit from the business. If you are married, both spouses must have jobs or be looking for jobs, or one spouse must be a full-time student or unable to care for him/herself.

Employers: Dependent care provided for your employees' families is deductible.

You can also pay employees money for them to spend on dependent care, tax free to the employees, up to $5,000/ year. You, the employer, get a deduction. You can take the deduction for your own family. Only if you offer the same assistance to your employees.

Child care business: Expenses for running a child care business are deductible like the expenses of any other business, including meals served to the children. If you run a child care business out of your home, see home expenses for the child care deduction allowed.

Deposits

Refundable deposits are not deductible.

Depreciation

Depreciation is an income tax deduction that allows a taxpayer to recover the cost of property or assets he/she purchased and "placed in service," meaning it is used in his trade or business. A fixed asset is an asset that a business or firm will use to earn income. In this situation, the owner of the business does not anticipate selling the asset within a year of acquiring it, but rather the asset will still be "in service" after that period of time and will help produce long-term income. Residential real estate can also be depreciated.

Examples of depreciable assets include:

- Machinery
- Vehicles
- Computers and software
- Other standard office equipment
- Furniture
- Buildings

Depreciation is contrasted with an expense. Business expenses, which commonly include cash transactions such as a business office supplies, are fully deductible in the year in which they were incurred. The expense of purchasing a fixed or tangible asset can be depreciated and spread out over a number of years.

Businesses have a choice as to how to take a depreciation deduction. They can either write the cost off as an expense or they can deduct it as depreciation. If the business chooses to write it off as an expense, they can deduct the entire cost in the first year. Or, they can depreciate it and write the asset's value off over its useful life expectancy. For example, if a business purchases a $70,000 piece of equipment, it can take the entire $70,000 in year one or deduct $10,000 a year for seven years.

Various types of property are subject to different periods of time over which they must be depreciated. Depreciation calculates how much of an asset's value will be "used up" over these periods of time. For example:

- Manufacturing tools and tractors depreciate over a period of three years.
- Computers, office equipment, light vehicles, and construction equipment depreciate over a period of five years.
- Office furniture and miscellaneous assets depreciate over a period of seven years.
- Residential real estate depreciates over a period of 27.5 years.
- Commercial real estate depreciates over a period of 39 years.

• Improvements to land depreciate over periods of 10, 15, or 20 years, with some exceptions.

Design Cost

Most design cost, including brochures, packages, and logos are deductible

Directors' Fees

Fees paid to directors of corporation are deductible

Disabled Access

Businesses that purchase equipment or devices, modify equipment or devices, or modify buildings or parking areas to make them more useable for disabled people are eligible for a Disabled Access Tax Credit.

Discounts

Discounts are not shown as an expense deduction. The lower sale price of your item is what is reported on the business tax return.

Dividends

When corporations distribute their profits to shareholders, these distributions are called dividends. Dividends are not considered business expenses and are not deductible. Cost associated with distributing dividends are deductible such as broker and bank fees.

Domain name

Expenses associated with acquiring, registering and keeping a domain name are deductible.

Donations

Only Corporations are allowed a deduction for donations to charities or community organizations, at least in the "Charitable" category. If the donation results in favorable publicity for the business, and therefore a likelihood of increased sales, many businesses deduct the donations, not as charitable contributions but as a promotion expense.

Downloads

Downloaded music, apps, software and publications, if for your business, are deductible.

Driveways

You can deduct the costs of maintain a private road or driveway on your business property.

Drones

Drones used for businesses can be deducted the year of purchase or depreciated over 7 years.

Drop shipping

Drop shipping is a business arrangement where your business contracts with another business to warehouse and ship products to your customers for you. The drop shipper may be the manufacturer, importer, or wholesaler of the products, selling the products to you but shipping them to your customer for you; or the drop shipper may be simply a warehouse and shipping service.

Goods that you have drop shipped for you are considered inventory event though you never have them in stock. You include the cost of the goods as part of cost of goods sold. Warehousing and shipping fees are also part of cost of goods sold.

Drug Testing

Drug test that are required by law, "Ordinary and "Necessary" are deductible

Dues for organizations

You may deduct costs for dues to professional organizations, and those organizations which you can show are necessary to conduct your business. For example, your dues to the Chamber of Commerce are deductible if you can show that your Chamber membership allows you to promote your business.

You may deduct dues you pay to:

- Boards of trade
- Business leagues
- Chambers of commerce
- Civic or public service organizations, like Kiwanis or Rotary
- Professional organizations such as bar associations and medical associations
- Real estate boards
- Trade associations
- Personal or hobby clubs

You cannot deduct dues for these types of clubs:

- Entertainment activities or facilities
- Recreation or sport, including golf clubs, country clubs, health and fitness clubs
- Airline or hotel clubs (like the airline clubs at airports)
- Any club with a social purpose

Education expenses

Self-employed business owners can deduct costs for their education, subject to certain limitations in the same way as individual taxpayers. You are self-employed if you own a business that is not a corporation.

To be deductible, you must be able to show that the education:

- "Maintains or improves skills required in your present work."
- It is required by law or regulations for maintaining a license to practice, status, or job. For example, professionals can deduct costs for continuing education.

Education expenses are not deductible if:

- The education is needed to meet the minimum educational requirements of your present trade or business. For example, you can't deduct the cost of obtaining a license to practice if you don't already hold such a license.
- The education is part of a program of study that will qualify you for a new trade or business.

Many employers provide educational benefits for employees. Some of these benefits are for continuing education, to maintain professional licenses, or to gain new skills, credentials, or degrees to benefit both the employee and employer. Self-employed business owners also may be able to deduct education expenses.

Education expenses are legitimate business expenses. But there are still some qualifications that must be met before these expenses are fully deductible to your business. As usual with the IRS, this issue is complicated. Consult your CPA.

Electricity

Electricity & Other utilities are deductible

Electronics

Electronic equipment and devices are considered business assets, which can be deducted the year of purchase or depreciated over 5 years.

Employee Business Expenses

If you reimburse your employee for out of pocket business expense, you are entitled to take a tax deduction for the expenses. There are strict rules surrounding employee reimbursement, consult your CPA.

Employees

Wages and benefits you pay to your employees are deductible.

Employment Agencies

As an employer, if you pay an agency to find you employees you are allowed to deduct the fees associated with the service.

Energy

The cost of using energy in a business is deductible in most cases.

Entertainment & Meals

The major change in business expense deductions in the tax law is the elimination of entertainment expenses, effective with the 2018 tax year. No more deductions for taking a client to a sporting event, concert, or resort.

Meal expenses are still deductible, with some changes.

- Meals during entertainment events are deductible if they can be separated out .
- Meals for employees while traveling, for all-employee events, or business meals, in general, are still deductible at 50 percent.
- Meals for employees at your location (think cafeteria or break room) are no longer deductible at 100 percent, but only at 50 percent).

Equipment

Equipment can be deducted the year of purchase or depreciated over fiver years or seven years, depending on the type of equipment.

Estimated taxes

The IRS requires Sole proprietors, Owners of LLCs, business owners to pay income and self-employment taxes in advance If the estimated combined taxes are $1,000 or more. C Corporations make quarterly tax prepayments if estimated federal income tax for the year is $500 or more. These estimated tax payments are not deductible expenses.

Exporting

All duties, tariffs, fees, and taxes related to exporting can be deducted.

Exterminator services

Deductible.

Family

A spouse or a parent on your payroll is treated like any other employee, expect a spouse and parents are not subject to Federal Unemployment (FUTA) Tax.

If you hire your children, if they are under the age of 18, they may be exempt from income and payroll taxes.

Finance Charges

Finance charges are usually deductible but there may be limitations. Consult your CPA.

Finder Fees

Finder Fees and commissions are deductible.

Fines

Fines and penalties for violations of the law are not deductible. Penalties relating to not meeting contract requirements, and any other fines and penalties that does not require breaking the law are deductible.

First Aid

Medical and emergency supplies are deductible.

Fixed Assets

Fixed assets are machinery, equipment, furniture, fixtures, and any other assets owned by the business are depreciable assets.

Fixed Cost

Fixed cost relates to the overhead expenses and all the various large and small expenses you pay whether you are generating income or not.

Fixing-up Expenses

Minor repairs to business property, building, and equipment are deductible as current expenses.

Fixtures

Shop, Store, and building fixtures can be deducted the year of purchase or depreciated over seven years.

Flexible spending accounts

A flexible spending account is an employee fringe benefit and is deductible.

Flowers

Did you know? Yes, flowers are deductible for your office, the store, secretary, client or customer.

Food

Food samples available to the public are fully deductible. Food served at business related events are deductible. Meals are partly deductible, see *Meals*

Free Agents

Free agents are another term for independent contractor and their fees are deductible.

Freelancers

Fees charged by freelancers and other independent professional are deductible.

Freight

Freight cost on goods you sell are deductible.

Fringe Benefits

Employers can deduct the cost of employee fringe benefits.

Fuel

All fuel costs are deductible. Fuel cost for cars and light trucks are deducted differently than large trucks and heavy-duty equipment. See *Automobiles*

Furniture

Furniture can be deducted in the year of purchase or the depreciated over seven years.

Garbage Services

Garbage services and other utilities are deductible.

Graphic Design

Deduction.

Grooming

Personal grooming expenses are not deductible, except when you're traveling away from home overnight on business.

Guard Dog

The cost of purchasing a guard dog can be deducted the year of purchase or depreciated over 7 years.

Gun

If having a gun is ordinary and necessary expense of your business, it is deductible.

Handling Charges

Similar to shipping, handling charges added to a freight bill are deducted.

Heating

Heating and other utilities are deductible.

Home Office

You can take a percentage of allowable home-related expenses, based on the percentage of your home used for business, including these expenses:

- Casualty losses (with limits)
- Mortgage interest
- Real estate taxes
- Security system
- Homeowner's insurance
- Direct expenses for improving the business area of your home
- Depreciation on your home's value
- Rent, if you don't own your home
- Repairs made to your work area or that benefit your work area
- Utilities

You can't include expenses for the home that have nothing to do with your business. For example, if you add a patio on the other side of your home, you can't include that in your deduction calculation.

Importing

All fees and taxes related to importing can be deducted.

Incorporation fees

If you are incorporating an existing business, fees to incorporate the business are deductible.

Independent Contractors

Independent contractors are not employees and are self-employed and in business for themselves. The cost of hiring an independent contractor is deductible.

Individual Retirement Arrangement (IRA)

IRA is a tax deferred retirement plan for individuals. Contribution to an IRA is not a deductible business expense.

Installment purchases

When purchasing business assets such as buildings, equipment, vehicles, furniture, fixtures, and machinery, you can deduct or depreciate the full cost, even though you haven't paid all of it yet.

Insurance

Insurance is deductible!

A typical business insurance policy will cover several types of coverage. The cost of these types of insurance is deductible business expenses. These coverages include:

- Property insurance, casualty insurance, and general liability insurance.

The casualty and liability sections deal with all kinds of employer liability, commercial auto liability, and general crime insurance.

- Business interruption insurance is often included with overall business property and casualty coverage. It includes coverage in case you can't carry on business after an unexpected emergency or natural disaster.

Other types of insurance that you may want to purchase for your business, and that you can deduct, include professional liability and malpractice insurance. If you have a service business or you give advice, you may want to consider errors and omissions coverage, a specific form of professional liability.

- Key person life insurance on company officers and executives. This

assumes that the company is the beneficiary, not someone like a spouse or other non-business person.

- Workers compensation insurance. Workers compensation is paid by the business to provide coverage for employees for on-the-job illnesses or injuries.
- Insurance on business-owned vehicles. You may only deduct the portion of the insurance premium applicable to business use of the vehicle.
- Group health care insurance coverage for employees, if your business

meets specific qualification requirements.

- Contributions to a state unemployment insurance fund, but the IRS requires that these payments must be "considered taxes under state law."
- If you have a home-based business, you may deduct a portion of the property insurance on your home that is related to your home office.

What You May Not Deduct for Business Insurance

You may not deduct the cost of life insurance for anyone associated with your company if you (the owner) are the direct or indirect beneficiary.

Business disability insurance for you as the business owner is tricky. If you deduct disability insurance premiums for yourself as the owner, then the benefits paid to you if you are disabled are considered taxable income to you.

As you Can tell Insurance is a complex subject, consult your CPA.

Intellectual property

Intangibles, also called intellectual property, are business assets you cannot see, such as copyrights, trademarks, patents, and goodwill. Most intangibles are amortized over a period of years.

Interest expense

Interest paid on business debts, interest on credit card purchases, and interest on purchases of business assets is deductible.

Internet

The cost of internet access is fully deductible if used only for business.

Inventory

Businesses that sell products need to be familiar with inventory. Keeping track of inventory is important for your business because:

- Inventory is a valuable business asset. You need to know how much you have and how much it's worth.
- Costs associated with buying and selling inventory are deductible business expenses that can reduce your business taxes.
- Reporting inventory correctly can keep you from having problems with the IRS.
- Cost and gross profit from sales of inventory is a major part of your business tax return.
- Did you know you can use the value of your inventory as collateral for a loan.

Businesses have two kinds of inventory:

- Supplies sitting on shelves waiting to be used.

These include office supplies, cleaning supplies, computer supplies and accessories, and supplies used for specific purposes, but not as part of your sales process.

•Product inventory can be products you purchase at wholesale to sell to consumers at retail. It can also be component parts or pieces or raw materials you use to make products to sell.

It's important to keep track of the cost of inventory items, so you know the profit on sales. This is easier said than done, depending on the type of product.

The most important thing to know about inventory is that it's essential in calculating the cost of goods sold (COGS). COGS is used to determine gross profit for a business that sells products, and it's used on every business tax form, for sole proprietorships, partnerships, LLC's, and corporations.

The Cost of Goods Sold Calculation is:

- Beginning inventory (the value of all inventory at the beginning of a year)
- Plus Net purchases (after discounts and allowances and returns)
- Equals Cost of Goods Available for Sale
- Less Ending Inventory (the value of all inventory at the end of a year).

A few more things you need to know about inventory and taxes:

- You must keep using the same inventory cost method over the years. You can't keep switching methods for the best tax advantage.
- Most important, remember to keep good track of your business's inventory to make sure you aren't losing any to theft, pilferage, or bad recordkeeping.

Janitorial service

Janitorial and cleaning services are deductible.

Land

Land is not deductible until you sell it. For deducting or depreciating the cost of a building, you separate the cost of a building from the cost of the land. Note, land improvements such as parking lots and major land scaping can be deducted or depreciated.

Landscaping

Landscaping, gardening, and lawn care expenses are deductible

Late Charges

Later charges incurred are deductible. However, penalties for late filing of government forms and tax returns are not deductible.

Laundry services

Laundry services for clothing used exclusively for work are deductible. Note, the clothing has to meet the IRS requirements. See *Clothing.* While traveling away from home on business, laundry service is deductible.

Lawsuits

The cost of a lawsuit is deductible in some situations and not in others. This topic is complex and you should consult with your CPA to ensure you are correctly deducting lawsuit cost correctly.

Money you pay for legal fees or court costs is deductible, as long as the legal matter is business and not personal. If you agree to pay the plaintiff to settle a civil suit, that's also a legitimate business write-off. If the government took you to court, you can write off any remedial or compensatory damages you pay. Fines and punitive damages are not deductible. Identifying which part of the settlement falls in which category is important for maximizing your deduction. you can't claim a business expense until you actually pay the money. A deal signed in December and paid in January is deductible on next year's taxes.

Lawyers

See *Professional services* and *Attorney.*

Leasehold Improvements

Leasehold improvements are components of a building that you are leasing that are not structural, such as portable air conditioning, fixtures, support for heavy machinery, partitions, and awnings. If you are a tenant and you are paying for leasehold improvements, you may be able to deduct them currently or you can depreciate them over 15 years.

Leases and Rent

Business leases and rentals for buildings, vehicles and equipment are deductible. Payments made to cancel a lease is also deductible

Car/Automobile Leases

There are limitations on car leases that are 30 days or longer.

Legal Fees

Most legal fees and paralegal fees, filing fees and related expense are deductible.

Licenses

Business licenses and permits, and licenses for any business property, are deductible.

Licensing Fees

Fees paid for the rights to use someone else's work, such as trademark or an artist's photograph are deductible.

List

Fees paid to rent or acquire mailing, email, telephone, or other lists are deductible

Loan Fees

Some loan fees are deductible. See *Loans* and *Interest*

Loans

A loan is not income when received and not an expense when paid. Repayment of a loan is not deductible. Interest, loan fees, and closing cost may be deductible.

Lodging

Lodging is deductible while you're traveling away from home overnight on business. See *Travel*. Corporations; can deduct actual lodging expenses or use a per diem rate. Non-corporate businesses; cannot use the per diem.

Logo

Cost of creating your company or product logo is deductible. Graphic designs and package designs are also deductible. Ask your CPA is the cost can be deducted immediately or has to be amortized over several years.

Losses

Casualty and theft losses are deductible, with some limitations. Business losses, which is shown as a loss on your tax return, can be used to offset other income this year and can also be used to offset profits from other years.

Machinery

Machinery can be deducted the year of purchase or depreciated over seven years.

Magazines

Magazines, books, newsletter, newspaper and all print and online publications that are in any way related to your business are deductible.

Mailbox store rentals

Mailbox store rents are deductible.

Mailing Lists

Mailing list rentals and purchase are deductible.

Mailing supplies and Expenses

Deductible.

Maintenance

Maintenance and minor repairs are deductible.

Makeup

See *Personal Appearance*

Management Fees

The fees charges by consultants you hire for management help are deductible.

Marketing

Marketing is a broad term that includes advertising, promotion, news releases, catalogs, public relations., etc. are deductible.

Market Research

Market research expenditures may be deductible currently, or they may have to capitalized over time if they are large expenses. If the expense is not substantial, the fees for market research are deducted when incurred.

Materials and Supplies

See *Supplies*

Meals

Meal expenses are still deductible, with some changes.

- Meals during entertainment events are deductible if they can be separated out

Meals for employees while traveling, for all-employee events, or business meals, in general, are still deductible at 50 percent.

- Meals for employees at your location (think cafeteria or break room) are no longer deductible at 100 percent, but only at 50 percent).

Taking these deductions is a three-step process:

First, you must verify that these expenses are legitimate business expenses. Some of these expenses are deductible, while others may not be. I'll explain more about what's deductible and what's not.

Second, you must have the documents to back up the deduction. You don't need to include these documents in your business tax return, but you will need them in case of an audit.

Finally, you must determine if you can take the full amount as a deduction or if the amounts are subject to the "50% rule," which limits the deduction to 50%.

More Guidelines on Deducting Meal Expenses

- The meal costs must be "ordinary and necessary" business expenses
- The costs may not be "lavish or extravagant"
- An employee of your company must be present at the meal
- If the meal is at an entertainment event, the meal must be separately priced,

Meals as business expenses must meet one of two tests:

- The *directly related test* applies if you can show that the main purpose of the activity was business.
- The associated test applies if the expense is associated with (along with, in conjunction with) a "substantial" business discussion. For example, if you had a meeting with clients at a restaurant and then you take the clients to the theater, this might satisfy the "associated" test.

You cannot deduct costs of meals for personal reasons while traveling. If the trip is "primarily" business, most expenses will be considered as business expenses. If the trip is "primarily" personal and you conduct some minimal business, only those costs directly related to the business you conduct may be deductible.

Because these expenses often happen while you are traveling, it may be difficult to keep good records, but it's important to record all details about the business purpose for these expenses. Note the business purpose on receipts, use an app, or take photos of receipts, and file all receipts so you can show them in case of an audit.

Medical expenses

Sole proprietors, partners in partnership, member/owners of LLCs, and owners of S-Corporations are not allowed a deduction for medical expenses for themselves or families. One exception to this rule is a medical expense or a drug test required by law for work, which is deductible.

Employers are allowed a full deduction for employees' medical expenses and for medical expenses of employees' spouses and dependents.

Meetings

Business Meetings are deductible. Although you are allowed only a 50% deduction for meals.

Membership Fees

Membership fees/dues and other expenses related to professional organizations, merchant and trade associations, unions, business leagues, unions, chamber of commerce and similar business groups are deductible.

Merchandise

Merchandise is another term for inventory, goods for sale. Merchandise cannot be deducted until sold.

Merchant association

Dues and meetings are deductible.

Messenger service

Messenger service are deductible.

Mileage Allowance

Mileage is deductible but there are rules to deducting mileage. Please read in its entirety.

There are two methods available for deducting driving expenses related to business travel, the standard mileage rate or the actual vehicle expenses.

What Is the Standard Mileage Rate?

The first option for deducting driving expenses is to use the standard mileage rate. In this deduction, you will calculate total miles driven and multiply it by the standard mileage rate.

Driving for Uber or another ride-sharing company? Driving for your own business? Driving a truck as an independent? No matter what kind of business driving you do, you need to know the IRS standard mileage rate for the year, in order to do your business taxes.

2018 Standard Mileage Rates is as follows:

- 54.5 cents per mile for business miles driven (up from 53.5 cents in 2017)
- 18 cents per mile driven for medical or moving purposes (up from 17 cents in 2017)

- 14 cents per mile driven in service of charitable organizations (fixed by Congress, never adjusted for inflation).

You can make deductions using standard mileage if:

- You have used the standard mileage rate since you first leased or bought the car.
- You have leased a car and intend to use the standard mileage rate deduction for the entirety of the lease
- You use four vehicles or fewer in your daily business operations.

You cannot use the standard mileage rate if:

- You have used the actual expense tax deduction and claimed the accelerated depreciation deduction in previous years.
- You have claimed a Section 179 deduction on the vehicle.

If you use the standard mileage rate you **cannot** *deduct:*

- Lease payments.
- Depreciation.
- Actual auto expenses.

You can *still deduct business related:*

- Parking fees and tolls.
- Interest if you have a loan on the car.
- Applicable registration fees and any taxes.

You can switch to using the actual expense method in later years even if you first began using the standard mileage rate.

Another option available for deducting driving related expenses is the actual expenses method. You can use this method if you are not able to use the standard mileage rate or if you simply choose not to.

You Must Use Actual Expenses If:

- You have a fleet of vehicles (more than four) used simultaneously for your business activities.
- You lease a car and do not plan on using the standard mileage rate for the entirety of the lease.
- You used the actual expense calculation when your vehicle was first used for business purposes. You cannot switch to standard mileage rate in later years.

Examples of Actual Expenses You Can Deduct:

- Interest on a vehicle loan
- Vehicle depreciation (leased vehicles cannot be depreciated)
- Registration fees and tax
- Parking fees and tolls
- Garage rent
- Lease payments (an income inclusion amount must be subtracted from the amount you can deduct if the vehicle's value is above a certain amount. This amount changes yearly so be sure to check with the IRS or your accountant.)
- Insurance
- Gasoline
- Oil
- Maintenance
- Repairs
- Insurance
- Tires
- License plates
- Registration fees

Mortgages

Mortgages on business property must be split into its components; Buildings, land, taxes, insurance, interest. Each component is classified in different categories.

Motorcycle

The cost of a motorcycle used for business can be deducted the year of purchase or depreciated over five years.

Moving expenses

You may deduct all the expenses of moving your business from one location to another. Employers can deduct moving expenses paid to employees or reimbursed to employees, if the move meets the IRS requirements for distance and length of the stay.

Musical Instruments & Equipment

If you are a singer, rapper, musician, band, or songwriter, the cost of your instruments and equipment can be deducted the year of purchase or over seven years.

Music System and streaming services

The office music system or subscriptions to streaming services can be deducted the year of purchase. The cost of music downloads, CD's, DVD's are also deductible.

Net Operating Loss

If your business incurs a loss this year, you will not owe any income taxes on the business. You may not know that this loss can be used to offset income and reduce taxes from other years. The loss can be carried back 2 years to offset income. If there are additional losses remaining you can carry the loss balance forward to apply to as many as 20 future years.

Networking

Networking usually refers to interacting with people to promote your business. Networking expenses are deductible, although you want to ensure that the expenses are not considered entertainment.

Notary Fees

Deductible.

Notes

Promissory Notes and notes payable, like loan payments, are not deductible. The Interest is deductible.

OASDI

"OASDI" Stands of Old Age, Survivors, and Disability Insurance. OASDI is another name for the combined Medicare and social security payroll taxes deducted from every employee's paycheck and collected from every employer. OASDI is also known as FICA. OASDI paid by employers on behalf of Employees is deductible.

Occupational

Occupational licenses, fees, registrations are deductible.

Office

Cost of renting an office is deductible. The cost of an office building you own can be depreciated.

Office supplies

Deductible, Deductible, Deductible!!!

Operating expenses

"Operating Expenses" is a general term for the day-to-day cost of running a business. Various expenses fall under this category, check individual category to determine if expense is deductible or not.

Operating Losses

Business losses can be used to offset other income in the year incurred and can also offset profits from other years, See *Net Operating Loss*

Organizational Cost

This is a tax deduction only available to corporations. Organizational cost are the legal and accounting services and government filling fees to set up a corporation. Up to $5,000 of the organizational cost can be deducted the 1st year the business opens. Expenses in excess of the $5,000 are amortized over 15 years.

Outside Contractors

Outside contractor and independent contractor are the same. Fees paid to outside contractors are deductible.

Outstanding Checks

Outstanding checks are checks that has been written that have not been deposited or cashed yet. You can deduct checks in the year they are written.

Overhead

Overhead refers to the fixed cost incurred by the business. Rent, utilities, phone, insurance, office supplies, Payroll, licenses, equipment and other assets. These costs cannot be directly tied to a product or service. Most overhead can be deducted, look up each category for guideline on how to deduct each expense.

Owner's Draw

The owner of an unincorporated business (Sole proprietorship, partnership, or LLC) cannot get a tax-deductible salary or wage. Payments to owners are known as "Draw"

Package Design Cost

Deductible.

Packaging Materials

Packages, bottles, boxes, cartons, packing supplies are deductible.

Painting

Paint Job is Deductible.

Paralegal Fees

Paralegal fees are deductible.

Parent on Payroll

If you hire your parents, they are considered regular employees subject to all regular employment and income taxes except federal unemployment tax (FUTA). Parents are exempt from FUTA tax. This does not apply to corporations. Family members employed by your corporation are treated like all other employees.

Parking

Parking at your regular place of work Is not deductible. This is considered a commuting expense. All other business parking cost are deductible.

Parking Lots

You can deduct the cost of maintain a parking lot or parking area on your business property.

Parking Tickets

Fines for breaking the law are not deductible.

Parties

A company or holiday party where all employees are invited is 100% deductible. All of your employees do not have to show up but they all must be invited to deduct the cost. Company parties that all employees are not invited to are considered entertainment therefore, not deductible.

Partners

Payments to partners in your business is not deductible. See *Paying yourself*.

Patents

Patent cost are amortized over 15 years.

Paying yourself

If your business is a sole proprietorship, partnership, or LLC, you , the owner (or co-owner), are not an employee of your business. You cannot hire yourself as an employee!!!! You cannot pay yourself a wage and deduct it as a business expense. You do not pay payroll taxes on it and you cannot claim it as a deduction. Your profit is your wage which is reported on your personal tax return.

Corporations: If your business is a corporation you are an employee of your business. Your salary is a deductible expense of your business. See *Wages*

Payroll

See *Wages*

Payroll Services

Hiring a payroll Service to process your payroll a deductible.

Penalties

Penalties for not meeting contract requirements, and any other penalties or fines that do not involve breaking the law are deductible.

Pension Plans

Pension plans are set up by employers for employees. Many employee pension plans are deductible, but you should consult your CPA.

Permits

Business Permits and Licenses are deductible. Permits obtained before starting your business cannot be deducted until the business is operating.

Personal Appearance

Generally, expenses incurred to enhance your personal appearance (Makeup, hair care, skin care) are not deductible, even if the expenses are incurred solely to present a business image. However, people who are in the business of selling makeup can deduct the cost of using those products on themselves, because they are modeling the product.

This deduction does not extend to clothing. You cannot deduct the cost of clothing for yourself even if you are in the business of selling clothing, unless the clothing is a costume, uniform, or clothing with your business name or logo on it.

Photocopies

Deductible.

Plants

Office plants and their upkeep are fully deductible.

Points

Points are loan fees and cannot be deducted immediately, they are spread over the length of the loan.

Postage

Postage, post office box rents, and postal permits are deductible.

Post Office Box

Post office box rent and mailbox store rents are deductible.

Presentations

The cost of planning and giving business presentations are deductible.

Prizes

Prizes and awards given to customers that generate sales or publicity for your business are deductible. There is a difference between prizes and gifts. Business gifts are limited to $25 per recipient per year. Prizes and awards do not have that limit.

Professional Services

The IRS specifically lists Certified Public accountants and attorneys under the category of legal and professional fees, but other professionals can be included. Such as, independent contractors, appraisers, systems analysts, consultants, and bookkeepers.

Fees paid to an attorney or accountant as part of the startup of your business cannot be considered in the category of legal and professional fees. These fees are part of the cost of business startup, and they must be included in this cost. Some of the cost of startup may be considered an expense in your first year of business, but the rest of these startup costs are spread out over several years. Some of these legal and professional fees for a business startup might include:

- Cost of hiring an accountant or consultant to set up your business accounting system and recordkeeping system
- Cost for an attorney to help you register your business legal entity with your state
- Cost for an attorney to set up your corporate records and prepare your bylaws, if you are starting as a corporation
- Cost for an attorney to write your partnership agreement for a partnership or operating agreement for an LLC.
- Some of these professional fees and costs are specifically not deductible as business costs, while others may be deductible in other places on your business tax return.

Fees paid to professionals for personal advice, personal taxes, or personal legal services are not deductible business expenses. Use your business checking account or business credit card for the business portion and your personal funds for the personal portion. You may not deduct fees paid to professional lobbyists to represent your company's interests in a local, state, or federal legislature.

Profit-Sharing Plans

Self-employed people cannot set up a profit-sharing plan for themselves, but they can have one or more retirement plans. Employers are able to deduct profit sharing plans for employees.

Promissory Notes

A promissory note is a promise to pay money you owe. The note is not deductible but the interest is.

Promoter fees

If you are a rapper, singer, musician, artist, or entertainer and you pay promoters out of pocket it is a deduction.

Promotion

Promotional expenses are deductible. These may include brochure, audio, public relations, small gifts, greeting cards, or some service.

Protective Gear

Cost of gear is deductible.

Raw Materials

Raw materials are a term used for the parts that go into your manufactured product. Raw materials are inventory and cannot be deducted until sold.

Real Estate

Real estate is a building and land. Buildings can be depreciated. Land cannot be written off until sold.

Rebates

Deductible.

Recreation Facilities and equipment

Recreation and athletic facilities and equipment on the business premises that are open to all employees are deductible.

Referrals

Commissions or fees paid for referrals are deductible.

Refunds

Money you refund to a customer is deductible.

Relocation Cost

Cost associated with relocating is deductible. See *Moving Expenses*

Remodeling

See *Building Improvements*

Rent

Rentals and leases for building, vehicles, and equipment are deductible.

Repairs

Minor repairs to buildings, machinery, and equipment are deductible are a current expense. Major repairs are deductible and depreciate over a period of years.

Research

Research and development cost are deductible.

Reserves

As reserves are funds set aside for future use or an unplanned expense or loss, it is not deductible.

Returned Goods

Refunds on returned goods are deducted from your income in figuring your taxes.

Rewards

Rewards to customers, vendors, and other nonemployees are deductible, within limits. See *Prizes*

Roads

You can deduct the cost of maintain a private road or driveway on your business property.

Robots

If used in your regular course of business, robots can be deducted the year of purchase or depreciated over seven years.

Royalties

Royalties you pay are deductible.

Safe

Safe can be deducted the year of purchase or depreciated over seven years.

Safe Deposit Box

Safe deposit boxes are deductible.

Safety Equipment

Safety equipment, first aid kits, fire extinguishers are deductible.

Sales Expenses

Most sales expenses are deductible. See individual expense category.

Sales Refunds

Money you refund to a customer is deductible.

Samples

Samples of your merchandise, given to prospective buyers or to people who might review or publicize your products are deductible.

Scholarships

Scholarship given to members of the community as a gesture of goodwill may be deductible as a promotional expense.

Security

Security services and patrols are deductible.

Seminars

The cost of attending seminars and business meetings are 100% deductible.

Service Contracts

Service contracts and extended warranties are deductible.

Service Mark

A service mark is a trademark that applies to a service. Service marks are amortized over a 15-year period.

Shipping & Shipping Supplies

Shipping and shipping supplies on goods sold are deductible.

Shoplifting Losses

Shoplifting losses are deductible as art of cost of goods sold.

Showroom

Cost of renting a showroom is deductible. If you are building your own showroom, you can depreciate over years.

Shows

If you put on a show to promote your business, the costs are deductible.

Sick Pay

You cannot deduct your own sick pay, unless you are an employee of your own corporation. Your employees sick pay is considered taxable wages; therefore, the expense is deductible.

Signs

Deductible.

Sponsorships

If you sponsor an event, individual, or team the expense is 100% deductible.

Spouse

Your girlfriend/ boyfriend is not considered a spouse. The IRS defines Spouse as anyone who is legally married. In many states, spouses are legally considered equal owners of all property and assets acquired by either spouse while married, including businesses. Even though one spouse may own the business, the other spouse can make business purchases and pay business bills. A Spouse is not able to deduct travel unless he or she is a partner or employee of the business.

Spouse as employee; you can hire your spouse as an employee of your business and get a payroll deduction like you would for any other employee. See *Wages*. Putting your spouse on the payroll will also make your spouse and family (including you) eligible for employee health insurance and medical expense coverage, all fully deductible. You will no longer be subject to the self- employed health insurance limitations.

Startup Costs

New businesses can deduct their costs for starting a business, but there are limits and restrictions on these costs.

The IRS says that start-up costs are "amount paid or incurred for

- Creating an active trade or business, or
- Investigating the creation or acquisition of an active trade or business."

Costs of starting a business can be separated into two time periods:

- costs for investigating and
- costs of start-up.

Business start-up costs are typically considered capital expenditures because they are for the long-term, not just the first year. That is, they are part of your investment in the business assets, and investment costs are amortized (spread out) over several years.

You may deduct up to $5,000 in start-up costs in your first year in business. This deduction is restricted if you have over $50,000 in start-up costs. If you have additional start-up costs over the $5,000, you can amortize these costs over 15 years. If you are not going to be profitable in your first year, you may want to consider another option to minimize your taxes in years where you make more profit.

Instead of deducting $5,000 in your first year, you may amortize all start-up costs over 15 years, taking the same deduction each year. For example, if your start-up costs are $15,000, you could deduct $1,000 a year for 15 years.

The IRS separates general business startup costs and organizational costs. Organizational costs are those costs involved in forming a corporation, partnership, or limited liability company (not a sole proprietorship). These costs must be incurred before the end of the first tax year the company is in business.

In addition to the $5,000 start-up deduction, you can take up to $5,000 in additional deduction for small business organizational expenses, up to $50,000. Let's say you have started an LLC in 2017. You have $10,000 in deductible startup costs and $2,000 in costs to set up the LLC. Here's how the deduction might work:

- You can deduct the $2,000 in LLC setup costs on your 2017 business tax return, as organizational expenses.
- You can also deduct $5,000 of your other startup costs on your 2017 taxes.
- The other $5,000 in startup costs must be amortized over the following few years, as required by the IRS.
- **Stationery**

Stationery, envelopes, and other office supplies can be deducted.

Stock

If you are buying a corporation and acquiring stock you may be able to deduct some of the cost. This is a complicated tax law and you should consult your CPA.

Storage Cost and facilities

Rent of a storage facility is deductible. The cost of a storage facility can be depreciated over time.

Store

The cost of renting a store is deductible. The cost of a building you purchase can be depreciated.

Studio

The cost of renting a studio is deductible and the cost of a building you own is depreciated.

Subcontractors

If you are hiring subcontractors to work with building contractors you are also hiring, you will deduct the cost the same you do building contractors.

Subscriptions

Subscriptions are deductible.

Supplies

Office supplies and miscellaneous business supplies are deductible.

Surveys

The cost of conducting surveys to get customers opinions is deductible.

SUVs

You can deduct the cost of using an SUV for business. See *Automobiles*

Tariffs

Tariffs and all fees and taxes related to importing and exporting can be deducted.

Tax Credit

Tax credits are special tax incentives created by congress to stimulate the economy, to encourage businesses to act in socially or environmentally responsible ways. Tax credits and tax deducts are different. Tax deductions are expenses that reduces business profit. Tax credits does not reduce your profit, it reduces your taxes directly.

Taxes

Most taxes other than federal income tax and self-employment tax are deductible. Below is a list of taxes that are deductible.

- Payroll Tax
- FICA Tax

- City or state gross receipts tax
- State unemployment insurance contributions and contributions to state disability funds (depending on the state)
- State income tax or state business franchise tax
- State, city, or local sales taxes you paid on business purchases
- Real estate tax or property tax on real estate owned by your business
- State income tax
- State unincorporated business tax
- Tangible and intangible property tax
- Customs, import, or tariff tax
- License tax (for your business license, city license, or other)
- Business vehicle registration tax
- Gasoline tax, depending on how you claim business mileage costs
- Telephone and cell phone taxes
- Taxes on business travel expenses, such as hotel taxes, air travel taxes, meal taxes, entertainment, laundry, etc.
- Excise taxes and fuel taxes
- Miscellaneous taxes on items like membership dues, stamps, safe deposit box rental, and others.
- Taxes on membership dues are deductible if the dues themselves are deductible. Only dues for business-related organizations are deductible.

Tax Penalties

Tax penalties are not deductible. Interest charges on late payments are deductible for corporations only.

Tax Return Preparation

Fees charged to prepare your business taxes are deducted. If your CPA is preparing your personal and business taxes ask him/her to separate out your bills for each service.

Telephone

All business telephone services, fees and taxes for landlines and cell phones are deductible.

Temporary Help Agency

Fees paid to temp agencies to aid in finding you employees are fully deductible.

Thank you cards

Deductible. It is such a nice touch to add to your product and/or service so now that you know it is deductible, send out a thank you card to your clients.

This Books

Yup, save your invoice and deduct it!

Tolls

Vehicle tolls are deductible.

Tools

Inexpensive tools and tools with a life of a year or less are deductible. Expensive tools are depreciated over seven years.

Tour Bus

If you are staying in a bus while traveling, your travel and living expenses are deductible.

Touring expenses

See *Travel*

Tractors

Tractors and construction equipment can be deducted the year of purchase or depreciated over seven years.

Trade dress

Trade dress is a form of trademark. The cost is amortized over 15 years.

Trademark

The cost of obtaining a trademark, service mark, trade name, or trade dress is amortized over 15 years.

Trade Show

Admission fees to trade shows are deductible. Travel and lodging/Hotel are deductible. Meal are 50% deduction.

Trailers

Travel trailers, utility trailers, and movable mobile homes can be deducted the year of purchase or depreciated over 5 years

Training

Training expenses, seminars, videos, and manuals are deductible.
See *educational expenses*.

Transportation

Local transportation expenses are deductible except commuting expenses which are not deductible. See *Commuting*.

Travel

If your travel is not commuting but is business travel, you can deduct travel expenses including:

- Transportation by airplane, train, bus, or car between your home and your business destination
- Taxi, uber, limo, or shuttle expenses
- Baggage fees or shipping of work-related materials
- Car expenses, for use of your own car or a rental car
- Lodging and meals, if your trip is overnight or long enough that you need to stop for sleep or rest
- Dry cleaning and laundry expenses
- Business-related phone calls while you are away
- Tips for business-related expenses while you are traveling
- Other business-related expenses while you are traveling.

It's important to keep good records on these expenses so you can show business purpose.

- Business Trips within the U.S
- Business Trips outside of the U.S
- Business & Vacation Combined
- Deductible Expenses

Trucks

You can deduct the cost of using a truck for business.

Tuition

Some tuition is deductible. See *Education*

Uncashed Checks

A check mailed or delivered by December 31 can be deducted the year it was written, even though it was not cashed until the new year.

Uncollectible Accounts

Uncollectable accounts are deductible as bad debts, but only if they were previously in your income when you made the sale.

Uniforms

Uniforms used exclusively for work are deductible. This includes costumes and protective gear.

Unions

Dues and meetings are deductible.

Utilities

Utilities, including electricity, gas, heating fuel, water, sewer service, and garbage pick up are deductible.

Vacation

Vacation Pay Vacation pay for employees is treated as regular taxable wages.

Vending Machines

Vending machines can be deducted the year of purchase or depreciated over seven years.

Voided Checks

If you void a check, you are not able to take a deduction.

Wages

The salaries, wages, commissions, and bonuses you have paid to the employees of your small business are tax-deductible expenses if they are deemed to be:

- Ordinary and necessary
- Reasonable in amount
- Paid for services actually provided, and
- Actually, paid or incurred in the year for which you claim the deduction

Warehouse

The cost of renting a warehouse is deductible. The cost of a building you own can be depreciated.

Warranties

Extended warranties that cost additional money are deductible if they do not extend beyond twelve months.

Water

Water and other utilities are deductible

Website

The cost of designing and setting up a website is deductible.

Work In process

"Work in process" also called "work in progress", is a manufacturing term for a product that is partially completed. Work in process is part of your inventory and cannot be deducted until sold.

Workshop

Cost of renting a workshop is deductible. The cost of a building you own can be depreciated.

This is a reference book that will help you identify potential tax deductions.

Choose your Tax Preparer wisely. Do your research and get vetted recommendations, search online reviews.

Never stop learning and investing in your mind.

www.ingramcontent.com/pod-product-compliance
Lightning Source LLC
LaVergne TN
LVHW061957070526
838199LV00060B/4173